# HABITATS

# DESERTS

JULIA WATERLOW

## Thomson Learning
### New York

# HABITATS

| | |
|---|---|
| Coasts | Mountains |
| Deserts | Polar Regions |
| Forests | Rivers and Lakes |
| Grasslands | Seas and Oceans |
| Islands | Wetlands |

**Cover:** An oasis and well in the Sahara in Algeria
**Title page:** Monument Valley, Arizona
**Contents page:** Herding camels in the Sudan desert

First published in the United States in 1996 by
Thomson Learning
New York, NY

Published in Great Britain in 1995 by Wayland (Publishers) Ltd.

U.S. copyright © 1996 Thomson Learning

U.K. copyright © 1995 Wayland (Publishers) Ltd.

Library of Congress Cataloging-in-Publication Data
Waterlow, Julia.
Deserts / Julia Waterlow.
      p.     cm.—(Habitats)
  Includes bibliographical references and index.
  Summary: Describes these arid lands through which some of the
world's largest rivers flow and explains how such areas are formed,
how they spread, and how life survives there.
  ISBN 1-56847-320-6 (hc)
  1. Deserts—Juvenile literature.  [1. Deserts.]  I. Title.
II. Series.
GB612.W38  1995
551.4'15—dc20                    95-30603

Printed in Italy

# CONTENTS

# 1. ARID LANDS

People often think of deserts as endless seas of sand, so unbearably hot and dry that no living creature can survive in them. Although it is true that deserts have little water and are inhospitable places for some species, they are certainly not all hot or sandy. Nor are they empty of life.

What makes a desert different from other habitats (places where plants and animals naturally grow and live) is the lack of rain. Deserts are areas with less than ten inches of rain a year or where evaporation of water, caused by high temperatures, is greater than rainfall. Some semiarid regions with between ten and twenty-five inches rainfall a year are like deserts because they lie in very hot parts of the world, and what little water there is evaporates quickly. The most arid parts of the world have less than one inch of rain per year and are known as hyperarid regions. However, nowhere on Earth is completely without rain.

The Sahara and the Australian desert, like the majority of the world's deserts, are hot. But altitude, the height above sea level, can affect desert

A rare sight in the Namib Desert in Africa: pools of water lie in hollows after sudden rain.

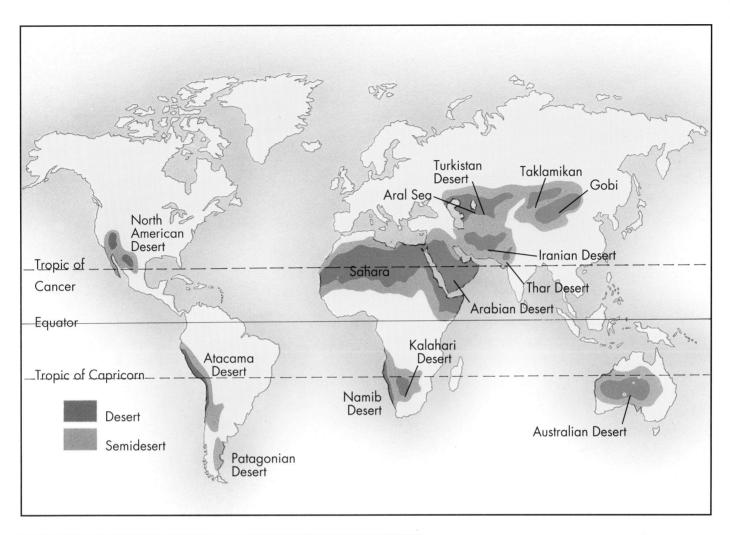

The map shows the world's deserts with labels: North American Desert, Sahara, Turkistan Desert, Aral Sea, Taklamikan, Gobi, Iranian Desert, Thar Desert, Arabian Desert, Atacama Desert, Kalahari Desert, Namib Desert, Patagonian Desert, Australian Desert. Reference lines: Tropic of Cancer, Equator, Tropic of Capricorn. Legend: Desert, Semidesert.

Most arid regions of the world lie close to the tropics of Cancer and Capricorn. Others lie far inland, cut off from rain-carrying winds by mountain ranges.

## Desert facts

- *About 30 percent of the world is covered in desert or semidesert, and some 13 percent of the world's population lives there.*
- *Largest desert in the world: the Sahara, covering an area of 3.5 million square miles.*
- *Hottest average yearly temperature in the shade: 94°F at Dallol, Ethiopia.*
- *Highest temperature ever recorded in the world: 136°F in Al Aziziyah, Libya, in Sahara (1922).*
- *Driest place in the world: Arica, Chile, where 0.03 inches of rain falls per year.*
- *Longest drought: Calama, Chile, where no rain fell for 400 years, until 1971.*
- *Largest single sand sea: Rub al Khali (Empty Quarter) in Arabia, covering 200,000 square miles.*
- *The Sahara produces between 60 million to 200 million tons of dust per year.*

temperatures. In regions of semidesert in Tibet, north of the Himalayas in Asia, the land lies mostly about 13,000 feet above sea level and temperatures often hover around freezing point.

Desert areas that are farther from the equator are also cooler. The semidesert of Patagonia at the southern tip of South America has an average temperature of only 45°F throughout the year.

Temperatures in deserts often vary by season. Tropical deserts, like much of the Sahara, see little change and tend to be hot all year round. Deserts in the middle of continents, such as the deserts of Central Asia and some of the deserts in the United States, can be bitterly cold in winter and searingly hot in summer.

Only about one fifth of the world's deserts have a sandy surface. The giant waves of sand dunes in the Rub al Khali (Empty Quarter) in Arabia are probably many people's image of a desert. However, most deserts are made up of stones, gravel, and rocks. For example, parts of the Gobi in northwest China have endless flat expanses of black and gray gravel with an occasional rock outcrop.

Deserts can be very beautiful, but of all this planet's habitats they are some of the least welcoming. Because of the lack of water or vegetation, animals and people are few and far between. Despite this, there is an amazing variety of plants and creatures that have adapted to such harsh conditions. Human beings have used their ingenuity to find ways to live in and even tame arid lands to suit their purposes.

A desert water hole in Rajasthan, India, provides a supply of water for people living in the region.

# 2. HOW DESERTS ARE FORMED

There are four main factors that contribute to the formation of deserts. Most of the world's deserts are the result of a mixture of these factors.

## High-pressure regions

Because the earth is round, its surface is not heated equally by the sun. Near the equator, where the sun's heat is greatest, the hot air rises, creating a zone of low air pressure. As the rising air cools, much of its moisture is lost as rain. The air spreads out from the equator and, at about 30° latitude north and south (around the tropics of Cancer and Capricorn), starts descending back to the earth.

The air begins to heat up again as it sinks, but, having lost most of its water, it is very dry. The sinking air produces areas of high pressure that block moist air from coming in and creates regions with very stable climates. It is in these high-pressure regions that most of the world's deserts are found. However, the deserts around the world at these latitudes are not all the same because wind patterns around continents break up the high-pressure belts in some places.

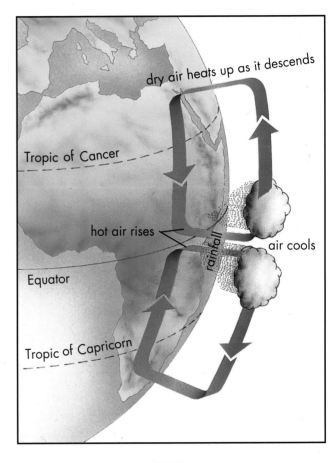

dry air heats up as it descends

Tropic of Cancer

hot air rises

air cools

rainfall

Equator

Tropic of Capricorn

**Above** Hot air rises at the equator, producing low pressure. It cools, loses moisture, and spreads at the tropics, resulting in warm and very dry high-pressure zones where deserts are often found.

**Left** In spite of very low rainfall, small bushes and shrubs manage to grow in the sands of the Simpson Desert in Australia.

Not all deserts are hot. In Asia, north of the Himalayas, there are high, dry plateaus over 13,000 feet above sea level. Temperatures in these desert regions often drop below freezing, and snow covers the surrounding peaks.

The Australian desert, the Kalahari and Namib Deserts in Africa, the Arabian Desert, the Atacama Desert in South America, and the Sonora Desert in California are all examples of deserts lying within these high-pressure zones. The largest desert on earth, the Sahara, with an area almost the size of the United States, is also in this high-pressure region.

The Sahara stretches west from the Red Sea for more than 3,000 miles to the Atlantic Ocean. This vast wilderness has a variety of landscapes, ranging from high mountains to wide plains and from rocky desert—stripped of sand and dust by winds—to large seas of sand dunes. The desert does not suddenly finish at the edges, except where it reaches the sea, but gradually turns into semi-desert where rain occasionally falls and patches of vegetation grow.

Some of the hottest temperatures on earth occur in the Sahara: during summer, temperatures can be over 130°F in the shade. However, temperatures vary over the Sahara's huge expanse, and on the northern fringes of the desert there is even an occasional frost in winter.

In all deserts there are great temperature variations between day and night. Because the air is so dry, there are few clouds over deserts. Clouds tend to hold heat in like a blanket; without cloud cover, heat soon radiates into the sky at night and temperatures quickly plummet, even to the freezing point.

### Desert rains

*Where rainfall is low, it tends to be unpredictable. It may fall in sudden storms over a very short time, or it may not fall for years, causing long periods of drought. For instance, in parts of Sudan on the edge of the Sahara, the average rainfall between 1965 and 1985 was 40 percent less than it was between 1920 to 1940; this drought caused terrible hardship for the people living in the area. Not knowing if or when rain will fall adds to the difficulties of surviving in arid lands.*

## Dry air currents

Most rain-carrying air currents come from across the sea, picking up water along the way. This moist air can travel quite a long way inland, dropping its moisture as rain. But by the time the air currents have reached the middle of continents, they will have lost all their moisture. These dry air currents create continental deserts.

Central Asia has some of the largest areas of continental desert. To the east these merge into the Gobi (Gobi means *waterless place* in Mongolian), which spreads across a large area of Mongolia and northern China. The Gobi is made up of several deserts including the Taklimakan, one of the most inhospitable and least explored sandy wastes in the world. Although in the Taklimakan a few seasonal rivers are fed from surrounding mountain ranges, they quickly disappear into the dry ground. Parts of the Gobi have dunes, as well as barren hills and plains of gravel and rock that look rather like a moonscape. Temperatures in continental deserts like this are extreme: in the Gobi, temperatures in July can reach 110°F and in winter fall as low as -40°F.

The Gobi lies in the heart of Central Asia, far from moist winds that bring rain from the sea.

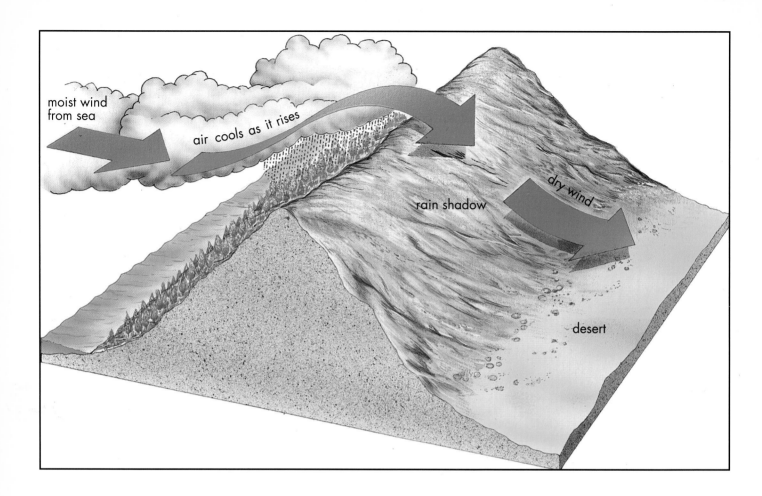

moist wind from sea

air cools as it rises

dry wind

rain shadow

desert

## Rain shadow

Some places are sheltered from rain-bearing winds by mountain ranges. As the air rises along the mountains, it cools and drops its moisture as rain or snow. By the time the air reaches the mountain range, it is dry, and deserts form in the rain shadow of the hills.

The dry basins of North America are examples of rain shadow deserts. A mountain wall is formed in the west by the Sierra Nevada of California and the Cascade Range of Oregon and Washington and in the east by the Rocky Mountains. Little rain is able to penetrate inland beyond these barriers. The dividing line between desert and nondesert can be very sharp. The spectacular desert basin of Death Valley, California, lies just east of the Sierra Nevada. Only 80 miles away, on the western, seaward side of the Sierra Nevada, is Sequoia National Park, with some of the largest trees in the world.

Rain-shadow deserts occur where mountains block rain-carrying winds.

## Comparing world rainfall (figures are average yearly rainfall in inches)

| 109 inches Belém (Brazil) | 95 inches Singapore (Malaysia) | 47 inches Sydney (Australia) | 42 inches New York (New York) | 24 inches London (U.K.) | 11 inches Alice Springs (Australia) | 9 inches Ulan Bator (Gobi) | 8 inches Karachi (Pakistan) | 3.5 inches Yuma (California) | 3.25 inches Kashi (China) | 1.5 inches Lima (Peru) | 0.1 inches Aswân (Egypt) |
|---|---|---|---|---|---|---|---|---|---|---|---|

## Cold ocean currents

Water is constantly circulating around the oceans as sea currents, which can be warm or cold. Water from polar regions sweeps toward the equator along the western coasts of continents. These cold currents cool the air, forcing it to drop its moisture over the sea; by the time winds reach the coast they are dry, and deserts may result. Moisture that reaches the coast turns to fog—a strange sight in a desert, but it occurs where warm air meets cold sea. The cold currents also cool air temperatures along the coast, though inland the desert becomes hotter and drier.

Deserts affected by cold ocean currents are the Sahara, the Atacama, and the Namib. Both the Atacama and the Namib Deserts are some of the most arid places on earth—until recently, the Atacama had received almost no rain for four hundred years.

**Above** Death Valley in California lies in the shadow of the Sierra Nevada. The annual rainfall here is less than two inches.

**Left** Fog caused by cold sea currents shrouds the Pan-American Highway as it winds through the Atacama Desert beside the Pacific Ocean.

11

# 3. NATURAL FORCES AND LANDFORMS

Desert landforms are the result of certain natural forces—wind, temperature changes, and water—that sculpt rocks and create strange features, many of them beautiful and spectacular.

## Wind

Winds are particularly powerful in deserts because there are few plants, especially trees, to break up the air flow or protect and bind the soil together. What little soil there is easily blows away.

The wind erodes rocks by whipping up sand and blasting it against the rocks. Over a long period of time, the wind has the same effect as continually rubbing a surface with sandpaper; it can cut away rock to leave strange forms shaped like pillars, mushrooms, and arches. Where the wind blows from one direction all year, a whole series of wind-eroded rocks or even hills, called *yardangs*, may be formed. A common desert feature is a

A wind-eroded rock in Death Valley, California

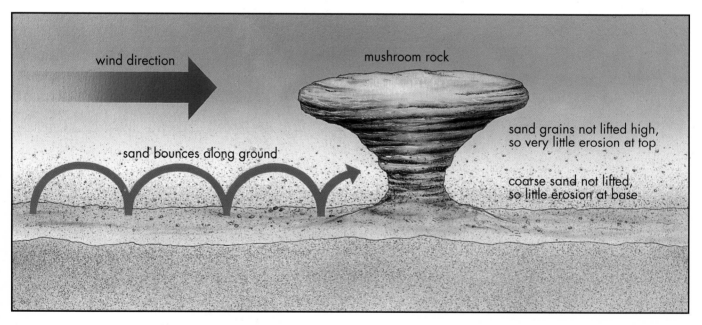

wind direction

mushroom rock

sand bounces along ground

sand grains not lifted high, so very little erosion at top

coarse sand not lifted, so little erosion at base

Desert sands are picked up by the wind and bounce along in the direction of the wind. This process is called saltation. Rocks in the wind's path are continually battered by particles of sand and are worn away to form strange, wind-eroded shapes.

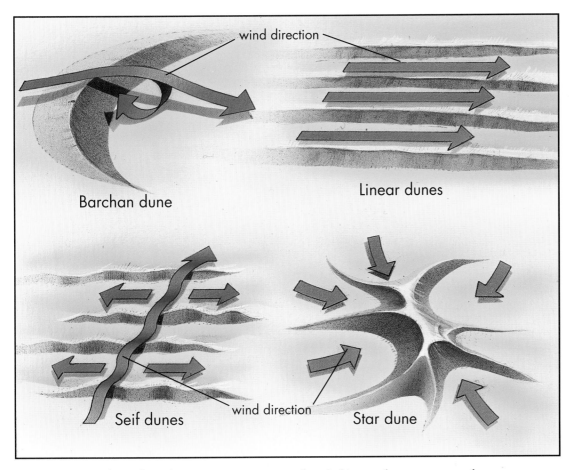

wind direction

Barchan dune

Linear dunes

Seif dunes

wind direction

Star dune

**Left** Dunes are heaps of sand. They come in all shapes and sizes depending on wind direction. Where wind blows from one direction all the time, long linear dunes are formed. Where there is an obstacle, moving crescent-shaped barchan dunes may form. Seif dunes have a curving course affected by crosswinds. Peaked star dunes may form where winds are variable.

stone-covered surface known as reg—in the Sahara, the reg extends over thousands of square miles. Wind erosion of sand and softer rocks leaves behind hard, resistant stones scattered across the landscape.

Sand itself is formed and shaped by wind—pieces of rock are gradually worn away until the hardest particles, usually made of the mineral quartz, are left. When blown, sand tends to collect in basins or pile up against anchored

**Left** Winds can blow dunes into rippling seas of sand.

objects or rocks. The different sizes and features of these dunes reflect the direction and force of the wind (see diagram page 13).

Dunes vary in size from 3 feet to over 1,000 feet high and more than 2,600 feet across. Driven by the wind, dunes are constantly creeping forward. Most advance about 20 to 30 feet a year and will slowly cover anything in their path. Large areas of dunes are named after the Arabic word *erg,* which means *sand seas,* because the wind blows them into a series of ripples like waves. The largest erg is the Rub al Khali in Arabia, but other large sand seas are found in the Sahara and the basins of Central Asia.

As well as sand, there is a massive amount of dust lying on desert surfaces. The wind sometimes whips this up into dust and sandstorms that fill the air and blot out the sun. Dust and sand find their way into everything. As well as being unpleasant for humans and animals, such storms damage crops and make it impossible to travel. Desert dust can be blown thousands of miles: red rain occasionally falls in northern Europe, which contains red dust blown from the Sahara.

Rocky deserts are more common than sandy deserts. In this part of the Namib Desert, winds have blown away light sand and dust, leaving heavier and harder rocks scattered on the ground.

14

## Temperature changes

The great variation in temperatures between day and night in most deserts causes rocks to expand and contract. This puts strain on weak points in the rocks, and they begin to fracture and crack, gradually breaking up. Occasionally rocks can be heard splitting apart with a sound like gunshot. Desert floors are often littered with shattered rocks. Sometimes lumps of harder rock, such as granite, are left sticking out of the surrounding weathered desert plain. These features are known as inselbergs. One famous inselberg is Ayers Rock, or Uluru, in Australia.

Salt lakes are unique desert features. Some, such as the Danakil Depression in Ethiopia, are the remains of dried-out seabeds. Others, such as the Great Salt Lake in Utah, are what remain of larger lakes when most of the water has evaporated in the hot desert temperatures. Groundwater is full of minerals and salts, but because only pure water evaporates, salts are left behind as a dry crust on the ground.

**Above** Ayers Rock, an enormous inselberg, stands out in the surrounding desert lands of the Northern Territories, Australia.

**Left** A salty crust is left on a dried-out riverbed in Death Valley, California.

## Water

It is strange to think of water creating desert features. Even though there is not much water, it can arrive suddenly in great quantities as torrents of rain or flash floods that disappear as quickly as they come. Such powerful bursts of water can erode the landscape with great force.

Arroyos (called wadis in other parts of the world) are valleys cut by sudden rushes of water. They dry up soon after rain stops. Where the rock is soft, water gouges deep grooves and ridges to form a landscape of strange shapes known as badlands. Earth and rock erode quickly in badlands, making it particularly difficult for any vegetation to take root.

Where rocks lie in horizontal layers, and some are harder than others, water erosion (with help from wind and weathering) can, over thousands of years,

The powerful force of water during sudden desert rainstorms can cut steep-sided valleys, or arroyos. The water quickly drains into the ground or evaporates into the air, and the arroyos soon become dry again.

produce features known as mesas
and buttes. A mesa is a large, flat-
topped island of rock that is left
standing when the surrounding
areas have been eroded away. When
these erode or weather further,
columns of rock called buttes
remain jutting out of the landscape.

Canyons are also formed where
rivers flow; for example, the world-
famous Grand Canyon was cut by
the Colorado River. The water has
sliced down into the rock and has
left almost vertical sides.

Fast-flowing streams caused by
sudden rainstorms have great power
and scour out huge amounts of
pebbles and rocks, which they carry

**Above** Mesas and buttes stand out in Monument Valley, Arizona. They are some of the oldest desert landforms.

**Below** Features caused by water erosion in some desert areas

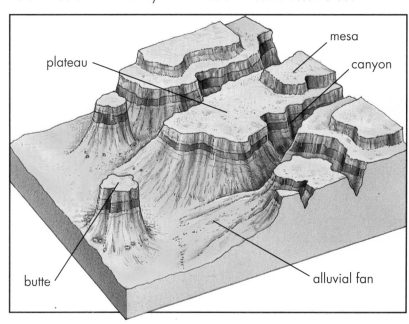

downhill. When they spill out of upland areas onto plains, the streams quickly slow down and, losing power, drop their heavy load. The water soaks away into the desert or evaporates, leaving fan-shaped deposits of coarse stone and rocks called alluvial fans. They can cover large areas and where several alluvial fans merge in a line they are called a *bajada*.

## Dust storms

Desert people have many local names for sandstorms and dust storms; they are called *haboob* and *khamsin* in the Sahara. There are also short-lived whirling columns of dust that spin randomly across the desert. Sometimes called dust devils, they are known as *djinns* in Arabia and willy-willies in Australia. Dust storms are more likely to occur in semi-desert areas and can be made worse by human activity. In the Sahel in Mauritania, on the southern edge of the Sahara, the land is gradually being stripped of its naturally sparse vegetation, causing the soil to become loose and unprotected. As a result there has been an increase in dust storms.

Dancers at a festival in Sudan are suddenly surrounded by a whirling dust storm that blots out the sun.

# 4. NATURAL DESERT LIFE

Deserts may seem empty of life, but amazing numbers of plants and animals have adapted to this mostly waterless habitat. The main objectives for both plants and animals are to find and conserve water and to avoid overheating, since many deserts have extremely high temperatures for much of the year.

## Plants

Plants need carbon dioxide to survive. Carbon dioxide is absorbed from the air through tiny pores, or holes, in the plant's outer layers, usually in the leaves. These pores, however, also allow moisture to evaporate, and in hot deserts most plants would soon dry out.

Some plants solve this problem by opening their pores only at night when it is cooler and water evaporates more slowly; other plants save moisture by having few

Many different types of cacti grow in the deserts of Mexico. Cacti survive in waterless places by storing water in their swollen, fleshy stems.

### Welwitschia

*The welwitschia, or tumboa, a plant found in the deserts of Namibia, is unlike most desert plants in that its long, straggly leaves have many pores. These pores are designed to soak up moisture from the frequent fogs that occur along the Namibian coast. Welwitschia can survive to a very great age—some are thought to be nearly two thousand years old.*

or small leaves. The cactus, a native plant of North and South America, copes by having no leaves at all. Its thick outer skin protects it from water loss and its few pores are tucked into shady parts of the plant.

The cactus also acts like a reservoir, storing water in its thick, swollen flesh. A large plant can hold as much as a ton of water after a rainstorm. However, its struggle to survive means that the cactus grows very slowly. The giant saguaro cactus can take forty years to put out a branch and may live for two hundred years.

The tough, leathery skin of plants like the cactus protects them from the harsh sunlight. Some plants have white hairs that reflect excess sunlight and act as a kind of insulation. The kokerboom tree of Namibia has not only a bulbous trunk that can store water, but also white bark that helps reflect sunlight. Another Namibian plant, the stone plant, camouflaged to look like stones, avoids excess heat by letting just the tip of the plant show above ground.

Desert plants are experts at finding ways to trap water. Some bushes, such as mesquite, have very long roots that can go down 50 feet to search for water.

**Above**
A kokerboom, or quiver, tree in the Namib Desert. It stores water in its thick, fibrous trunk, and the waxy coating on its bark helps to stop water loss.

**Left** Desert flowers burst into life after rain. The blossom will produce seed and die within a few days.

On the other hand, plants such as the creosote bush and some cacti have shallow roots that spread over a wide area, so they can easily absorb water from dew or brief showers. The creosote bush is one of many plants that have adapted to desert conditions by becoming tolerant of long periods of drought; it is able to survive up to a year without rain. Storing water underground in thick, bulbous roots is another survival technique of some plants.

But most desert plants have no way of surviving droughts. Instead, they produce seeds that stay dormant until it rains; then suddenly a carpet of flowers such as poppies and rockroses covers the desert. The plants appear in a quick burst of growth, going through their life cycles in a matter of days and scattering their seeds before they die. Seeds that have lain dormant for three hundred years have been known to grow and flower.

## Insects, spiders, and scorpions

Many varieties of insects manage to survive in deserts because their hard shells or skins protect them from water loss and overheating. Like other desert animals, insects tend to be active at night; during the heat of the day, they either burrow into the ground or shelter in the shade of rocks. Some insects get water from their prey; some rely on other sources. The darkling beetle of Namibia drinks dew that forms on its body early in the morning. The honey ant of the southern United States and Australia has a stomach that swells to many times the size of its head; here it stores food and liquid for times of drought.

Scorpions cope especially well. Although they are protected from the sun by a hard shell, scorpions tend to stay hidden until the cool of evening when they come out to hunt. They kill insects and spiders with a sting from their tails; some scorpions have poison that is strong enough to kill humans. Scorpions have no need to drink because they get all the water they need from eating their prey.

Scorpions usually shelter under rocks in the heat of the day and come out at night to hunt.

The young need to be protected from the heat, and insects and spiders have developed ways to do this. The scarab beetle lays its eggs in pieces of animal dung and buries them in the sand; the Australian desert wolf spider keeps the egg sac attached to its body so that it is shaded from the sun. Most desert spiders do not make webs to trap insects, for there are not many small flying creatures in deserts.

## Reptiles and amphibians

Most desert snakes are nocturnal. Lizards, the most common desert reptiles, tend to be active during the day, though not at the hottest times. Their scaly skin helps them retain moisture, which is provided by their prey.

In order to travel across extremely hot sand, some reptiles have developed special ways of moving. The sidewinder snake slithers sideways, allowing only part of its body to touch the sand at any one time. Desert geckos often have either fringelike hairs around their feet or webs between their toes to keep them from sinking into the sand.

**Above**
A sidewinder slithers quickly down a sand dune. Its sideways movement helps it travel easily over the soft sand.

**Left** Desert creatures have many ways to frighten off predators. Some are camouflaged so that they blend into their surroundings. Others, like this Australian horned devil lizard, look fierce.

Incredibly enough, there are even amphibians that survive in the desert. The spadefoot toad of North America buries itself between rains and goes into a kind of hibernation called estivation. The toad can survive for as long as nine months on its fat reserves. When it hears the sound of the rain falling, it emerges and lays its eggs in pools of rainwater.

## Birds

Birds need to drink water on a regular basis, but at least they can fly to find it. The sandgrouse travels up to 30 miles a day to fetch water for its young in the nest; it brings the water back in its feathers, which are soaked like a sponge. The sandgrouse's nest (and the ostrich's) is on the ground, because there are few trees and bushes to use as nesting sites. In the United States, the gila woodpecker makes a safe nest by pecking a hole in the saguaro cactus; the fruit of the cactus also provides the woodpecker with food and water. Hawks, falcons, and vultures are also found in deserts, hunting other birds and small mammals that provide them with water as well as food.

**Above** Some toads and frogs manage to live in desert sands. They come out to lay their eggs after a rainstorm leaves puddles in which tadpoles can grow.

**Left** Without trees, there are few safe nesting places in desert areas. Some birds nest on the ground. Others, like this cactus wren, in the Sonora Desert in California, tuck their nests away among the spines of cactus plants.

## Mammals

Because there is little shade, small mammals such as mice, gerbils, hamsters, desert kangaroo rats, and the North African hedgehog burrow to protect themselves from the extremes of temperature. They stay underground during the day and come out when it is cooler to search for food such as seeds. To reduce water loss they do not pant or sweat and their urine is highly concentrated. Their fur helps insulate them from the heat; although dwarf hamsters, which live in the cold deserts of Central Asia, have thick fur to keep them warm.

Slightly larger mammals such as foxes and meerkats also burrow. The fennec fox of the Sahara hunts in the evening for insects, lizards, and small mammals. It has enormous ears that not only assist in tracking prey but also help the fox lose heat and cool down. The African ground squirrel has another way of keeping the sun off—it holds its bushy tail over its head like a parasol while searching for food.

Big mammals are rarer because of the scarcity of food and water, but several kinds of gazelles and antelopes manage to survive off scanty grass. Most are found in African deserts. Those of the Sahara have been hunted almost to extinction. Other animals found in desert areas include camels and wild asses in central Asia and kangaroos and wallabies in Australia.

**Above** African ground squirrels make their homes in burrows under the rocky desert. They come out to search for seeds.

**Left** The oryx is one of the few larger mammals that manage to live successfully in deserts. The oryx often has to travel many miles to find water, but it can survive by feeding on tussocks of grass and even thorny shrubs.

24

# 5. WATER IN DESERTS

Although rainfall is rare or infrequent in the desert, there are other sources of groundwater, such as rivers and aquifers. A place with sufficient water to allow plants to grow in an otherwise barren desert is called an oasis.

## Rivers

Surprisingly some of the world's largest rivers flow through deserts. All of them have sources of water far away where rainfall is higher, usually in mountains. Some well-known rivers that pass through deserts include the Nile, the Niger, the Tigris and Euphrates, the Murray and Darling, the Rio Grande, the Colorado, the Indus, and the Yellow rivers. These rivers are often the only source of water available in the desert, so people are very dependent on them. Many great past civilizations have developed along desert rivers.

Fields in the eastern part of the Sahara are irrigated by water from the Nile. This has helped farmers grow crops in the desert for more than six thousand years.

### Water control
*All over the world, countries with large areas of desert are looking for sources of water to make the land productive. Conflicts arise especially where a river flows through two countries that need its waters. In Africa, the Nile first flows through Sudan and then on into Egypt. The two countries have agreements on how much water each can take; but Sudan's requirements are growing, and this could lead to problems for Egypt.*

A dam holds back the Colorado River, creating a huge reservoir of water. From here water is piped for use in homes, farms, and industries in the deserts of Arizona.

Complex methods of irrigation have been devised to move river water into deserts for irrigation and other uses. In richer countries, mechanical pumps are used to feed water into channels or pipes that radiate out from the river and supplying farms, homes, and industries. Water from the Colorado River is completely controlled with dams and aqueducts that transfer water hundreds of miles to the deserts of California and Arizona. Less developed countries, such as Egypt, still use traditional methods that do not require expensive machinery or fuel, as well as modern dams and pumps.

Flowing through the deserts of Iran, the Middle East, and western China are extraordinary underground channels called *qanats,* or *karez.* People have

A *karez,* or underground canal, is a method used in some deserts to bring water to an oasis. Being underground, the water does not evaporate in the hot sun.

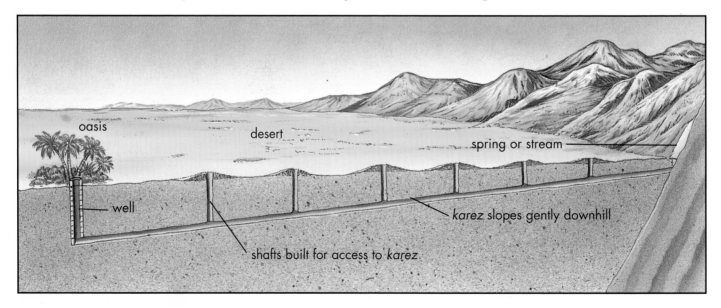

oasis

desert

spring or stream

well

karez slopes gently downhill

shafts built for access to *karez*

tunneled them under deserts to bring water from nearby mountains to supply oases. Even though it may have traveled many miles under hot sand, the water can still feel ice cold when it reaches the oasis. If the channels were out in the open air, the water would easily evaporate. The huge Iranian system, with more than 150,000 miles of channels, was begun by the Persians in the seventh century B.C.

Irrigation must be carefully controlled. Most soils contain salts, which, if they become too concentrated, will prevent plants from growing. In places with heavy rainfall these salts are regularly washed away, but because of low rainfall, some desert soils suffer from excess salt. When irrigation water is applied in large amounts without proper drainage, the water table in the ground can rise and bring salts

**Above** Urged on by a boy, a harnessed donkey walks around in a circle, turning a wheel that pumps water onto fields. This simple method has been used for hundreds of years.

**Left** By using large-scale modern irrigation methods, wealthy countries can turn the driest desert regions into productive farmland. These huge sprinklers are watering fields using water pumped from an underground aquifer (see page 29).

close to the surface, where they damage crop roots. Where irrigation water evaporates, a white crust of salt is left on the fields. This process, called salinization, is thought to be happening in as much as 30 percent of the world's irrigated desert areas.

It is particularly serious for Egypt, since nearly all the population live in the Nile valley and depend on its produce. Between 30 and 40 percent of the irrigated land is affected by salinization. There is a lesson to be learned from the past: in Iraq thousands of years ago, salinization, due to large-scale irrigation projects, helped bring about the end of the great Mesopotamian civilization.

The bare white patch in this Egyptian field is where salt, naturally present in the earth, has been brought up to the surface by applying too much irrigation water without proper drainage. Plants will not grow in soil that contains a lot of salt.

### The Aral Sea

*The deserts of Central Asia are crossed by two large rivers that flow northwest to the inland Aral Sea. Using the waters of these rivers, huge areas of arid land have been irrigated for agriculture; but the consequence has been the upset in the balance between inflow and evaporation in the Aral Sea. Between 1960 and 1990 the sea shrank by about 40 percent and is still getting smaller. Its waters have become so salty that fish are dying, and the dry, salty winds are having unpleasant side effects on humans. Towns that were once ports are now far from the sea, and fishermen can no longer make a living.*

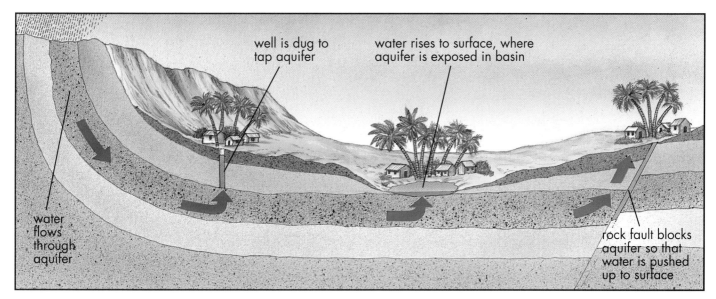

In the diagram:
- well is dug to tap aquifer
- water rises to surface, where aquifer is exposed in basin
- water flows through aquifer
- rock fault blocks aquifer so that water is pushed up to surface

**Above** How aquifer water can reach the surface

## Aquifers

An aquifer is an underground layer or reservoir of water-filled rock. The water lies in pores or spaces in rocks, or in the joints between rocks, and may have taken many thousands of years to accumulate. Some are continually recharged with water that seeps through underground, but many aquifers take a long time to fill up again once the water is used up. In some cases, the aquifer may never be recharged.

Water tends to flow through aquifer rocks and can surface naturally, sometimes in a basin or perhaps where a fault in rock forces water upward (see diagram above). If the water does not flow to the surface, people tap it by drilling a well or pumping it to the surface. Modern pumps can bring water to the surface from as far as 1,500 feet underground. As long as the underground water is not too salty or full of minerals, the oasis fed by the aquifer can support plants, animals, and people.

It is expensive to pump water from far belowground, so it is mainly rich countries such as the United States that use this type of water source on a large scale in deserts. In Texas, Colorado, Arizona, and California, huge quantities of water have been extracted from aquifers to irrigate crops and to serve desert city dwellers. However, the aquifers are being drained more quickly than they can recharge, leading to a rapid decline in levels of underground water. It is likely that the water will eventually run out.

**Below** Wind pumps are often used to bring underground water to the surface. This wind pump in the Namib Desert National Park is used to supply a water hole for wild animals such as the oryx.

# 6. LIVING OFF THE DESERT

## Hunters and gatherers

Hunting and gathering are among the oldest ways humans have managed to survive in arid places, but today not many people live this way. Certain groups of San Bushmen in the Kalahari Desert and Aborigines in the Australian desert are among the few hunter-gatherers left.

These people must know their land inside out to get enough water and food. The Bushmen are skilled at finding edible berries and seeds and fleshy roots that contain water and are often the only source of water in the driest months. Wild game also provides food; uneaten chunks of meat are cut into strips and dried so that they will keep for future use. Like the Bushmen, Aborigines recognize where water, plants, and animals can be found. These hunter-gatherers are always on the move, for the longer they stay in one place, the harder it becomes to find food.

A woman of the San tribe uses a stick to dig up an edible root from the sandy soil of the Kalahari Desert. This is the traditional way that the San of the Kalahari find their food and water in very dry desert regions.

Most Aborigines of Australia no longer live nomadic lives, hunting and gathering. Their land has been taken for farming, and they have been forced to find other ways to live. These Aborigines make a living by painting their native designs on cloth for sale to tourists.

## Herding animals

Raising animals is difficult in very arid places, but where there are seasonal rains or a scattering of oases it is possible. Desert herders most commonly keep flocks of camels, goats, and sheep that manage to live off poor pasture. Traditional herders, like hunter-gatherers, lead nomadic lives, moving with the seasons to find new grazing land for the animals.

Cattle, too, are raised on many desert margins, such as the edges of the Kalahari and Sahara. Some are herded in the traditional manner by nomadic people, who reduce the number of cattle during the dry season or during droughts. Nowadays, however, deep wells can be dug to provide water, so cattle are raised on huge ranches. As a result, the land may become overgrazed, and the animals have to be fed on fodder brought from elsewhere.

31

**Left** In the Sahara on the borders of Egypt and Sudan, people raise herds of camels and take them to sell or trade at markets in the Nile valley.

**Right** Navajos tend sheep in the arid hills of the Arizona Desert.

Traditional herders depend on their animals for most of their needs. The Tuareg people of the Sahara live off the milk and meat of camels and goats; they use their hides to make such things as tents and water containers. In the Gobi, the Khalkha Mongols keep sheep, goats, and a few hardy two-humped Bactrian camels for food (mostly butter and cheese made from the animals' milk), as beasts of burden, and for trading. The number of people in each group of herders is small and they are constantly on the move, so they do not overstretch the resources of the desert.

## Crops

Growing crops in deserts depends mostly on irrigation. Oases with plenty of water can produce excellent crops; the sunshine helps fruit and vegetables to grow particularly well. A tree commonly planted in hot desert oases is the date palm, which is used not only for its fruit but also as a building material.

On desert margins some farmers depend on seasonal rains. At the minimum, there needs to be about eight inches of rain a year to farm without extra irrigation. Crops planted just before the rains are called catch crops and are usually staple foods, such as barley, wheat, millet, corn, and vegetables. Droughts can be a disaster, leaving the young plants dying and the people without their yearly crop of food.

**Date palm**
*The date palm can grow in soils that are too salty for many other plants, so it is a valuable tree for oasis dwellers. Dates, the tree's sugary fruit, can be eaten raw, cooked, or dried. The leaves are used for fodder, to make rope, and as a roofing material; the trunks provide wood for building and fuel.*

Massive amounts of water are diverted from the Nile to irrigate sugarcane fields in Sudan. The sugar is sold as a cash crop, but in such a dry region, with so many poor people, the irrigated land might be better used to grow food.

# Greening the deserts

Large tracts of desert have been reclaimed for farming in developed countries, where people can afford the high cost of irrigation. In Utah, for example, where water was once brought by mule, some 40 million acres are now irrigated. Parts of southern California that were previously desert are today major food-producing regions. Extensive irrigation has also made farming possible in many deserts of the Middle East; for example, in the Negev Desert in Israel, luxury vegetables are produced even in winter.

If the source of water is not renewable, such as a slow-filling aquifer, this kind of agriculture is not really economical or sensible in the long term. Water in deserts in the United States is now having to be pumped from greater and greater depths as aquifers run dry, and the costs are becoming too high for many farmers. It has also been found that when the water table is lowered too much, saltwater is drawn into the aquifer, making it unusable. In other places, the land has subsided (sunk) several yards where water has been taken out. It is quite likely that unless other sources of water are found, reclaimed land will become desert again.

Irrigating deserts ought to bring benefits to the people who live and depend on the area. In some poorer countries, newly irrigated land is bought up by richer farmers to grow cash crops. In Sudan, a dam project on the Nile enabled a huge area, known as Gezira, to be irrigated. This area could have helped produce more food, but mostly sugarcane and cotton were planted, and the profits went to a few rich landowners. Even during Sudan's famine of 1984, when thousands were starving, cotton was still being harvested.

This irrigation system uses an electric pump to raise water from an aquifer and feed it into a huge moving sprinkler. This circles around, spraying water on desert lands so that they can be cultivated for crops.

# 7. SURVIVAL IN THE DESERT

Camel caravans are among the most ancient ways of traveling in deserts. They can still be seen in some parts of the Sahara and Central Asia. This caravan is crossing the deserts of Ethiopia.

## Travelers

Deserts are barriers to travel because of the problems of survival in the harsh environment. One of the first reasons people tried to cross deserts was to trade. Usually they would travel in groups called caravans. Traveling together provided protection against raiders, and it was also safer in such severe weather conditions. Trade routes crossed deserts from oasis to oasis, where travelers could replenish water supplies. Many traders were desert people themselves, either from oasis settlements or groups of nomadic herders.

Crossing the desert was a great challenge for adventurous explorers. The great Arab scholar and explorer Ibn Battuta crossed

### Desert victims

*The first crossing of Australia from south to north and through the deserts of the interior was led by two inexperienced men, Robert Burke and William Wills. On the return journey, after killing their camels for meat, they ran out of food and water. Both Burke and Wills died of starvation and exhaustion, and only one member of the team survived, helped by local Aborigines.*

the Sahara to Timbuktu in the fourteenth century, almost dying of thirst on the way. From the fifteenth century on, desert explorers were mostly Europeans. At first they came as missionaries and traders, then later as adventurers and scientists who were curious to find out about the vast, seemingly empty open spaces that did not exist in Europe. Their inexperience led many to die of heat, thirst, and starvation, but others took along local guides who showed them ways to survive.

A jeep, the modern version of a camel, carries people through the Namib Desert. Although faster than camels, jeeps can get stuck in soft, deep sand.

Traveling in deserts today is far simpler, for there are now roads, even across the Sahara, and airplanes to reach remote places. Inventions such as air conditioning, sunscreen, and plastic water containers make journeys easier and more comfortable. However, even jeeps can get stuck in the sand, water can run out, and sandstorms can make it impossible to find the way. Desert journeys will always be risky adventures.

### "Ships of the desert"

*Although there are now roads crossing many deserts, camels are still used for transportation, especially in the Sahara and the deserts of Central Asia and China. Sometimes called "ships of the desert," camels are ideal desert vehicles. They can survive for up to ten days without water, living on tough desert plants. Their broad feet prevent them from sinking into soft sand. Their long eyelashes keep sand from blowing into their eyes, and their ability to close their nostrils also helps to keep out blowing sand. A camel's hump is mostly fat, which can keep the animal going for days without food.*

Nomadic Berbers in the Sahara. Their tented homes, made from cloth or hides, are ideal for their lifestyle: the tents allow cooling breezes through and can be packed easily when the Berbers need to move on.

## Homes in the desert

One of the oldest and most densely inhabited areas of desert is the Nile valley. Other desert river valleys and isolated oases have also been settled for many centuries, flourishing on desert trade routes. The remote Tuareg settlement of Timbuktu, situated on a trans-Saharan caravan route, thrived for many years as a trading point for gold, salt, and slaves. Many of the oases along the ancient trade route in China known as the Silk Road are still busy settlements today.

Building materials are scarce in the desert. Evidence from the Sahara and the Middle East show that desert people originally lived in caves. Now they have permanent buildings, often made of mud or clay bricks. Thick walls provide insulation from the heat (and the cold at night) and are often painted white, which helps reflect the sun's rays. Where there is no rain, such houses can last for years.

Nomadic desert people need portable shelter, so many, such as the Bedouin of Saudi Arabia and the Mongols of the Gobi, use tents.

## New ways of life

Life has changed for all desert people over the last 50 years and traditional ways are fast disappearing. Desert life is harsh, and people can now find easier ways of making a living. In the 1950s about 20 percent of Bedouin were still

### Dressing for the desert

*Desert peoples have religions and customs that influence the kind of clothes they wear, but most have a practical use, too. The Tuareg dress in layers of loose garments that protect them against the heat and allow air to flow round. Headgear is essential as a shield from the sun, and veils can keep out dust and sand in storms. Sandals protect the feet from hot sand.*

nomads; now they number less than 3 percent. Others, such as the San of the Kalahari Desert and the Aborigines of the Australian Outback, have been driven off their desert lands by ranching and mineral exploitation and have ended up struggling to survive in the modern world at the lowest level of society, often in great poverty.

In some wealthy countries people are doing the reverse; they are moving into the desert because modern water technology has made it possible to create artificial oases. Phoenix, Arizona, for example, is a desert city of houses with lawns, trees, and swimming pools where the heat is made bearable by air conditioning. The huge populations of cities like this are totally dependent on artificial water supplies brought up from below ground or piped in from sources far away.

# 8. RICHES OF THE DESERT

Laying a new oil pipeline in the Middle East. The deserts of this part of the world are especially rich in oil.

## Oil, gas, and minerals

The most valuable desert products today are crude oil and natural gas. Desert regions once had different climates and were covered in forests and swamps that, over millions of years, decomposed. As they were squashed into layers of rock by earth movements, fossil fuels such as oil and gas were formed. Now these rich reserves are tapped by drilling into porous rocks where the oil and gas lie, sometimes over two miles down.

Although there are oil and gas deposits in many parts of the world, those in deserts are often the easiest to exploit. It may be very expensive to set up a base in the desert because of the supplies that have to be brought in, but the land is cheap and usually easy to survey. There are few other industries and few people who might be affected by or complain about the noise, mess, and pollution that can result.

Finding a rich deposit has brought fabulous wealth to desert countries that might otherwise have been poor. This has happened to countries in the Middle East such as Saudi Arabia and Kuwait, which are thought to have nearly 70 percent of the world's oil. Neighboring countries

### Salt
*One of the most ancient desert products is salt. It used to be a valuable commodity for caravan traders and is still mined from salt lakes in many deserts of the world. In the Danakil Depression in Ethiopia, thick layers of salt left by evaporation of water are carved out by hand and carried in slabs by camels to a salt market more than 50 miles away.*

39

benefit too; for example, about 20 percent of Egypt's wealth comes from Egyptians working in Saudi Arabia. For the people of oil-rich countries, life has changed from simple herding and farming to modern urban living in just a few years.

Many other countries also drill for oil and gas and mine minerals and precious stones in desert regions. The deserts of the United States and Chile have huge copper mines; the Sahara has deposits of iron ore and phosphates; and South African mines produce precious metals and stones such as gold and diamonds. Australian deserts are rich in every kind of mineral. But surprisingly, the largest excavations in deserts are for rocks, gravel, and sand, used for constructing roads and buildings.

**Above** The world's largest uranium strip mine lies in the Namib Desert. Water, food, and fuel for the mine and the workers have to be brought here across the desert.

Minerals are nonrenewable resources and will not last forever. In the United States, it is thought that oil fields may run out within ten to twenty years. Unless the money made from mining is used to develop other industries, huge numbers of people could be left unemployed in the future.

There are also effects on the landscape to consider. Huge scars are left from strip-mining, and mounds of rock and earth are dumped across the desert. Deserts do not recover as easily as other habitats because there is no rain to wash away the mining scars or to encourage vegetation to grow back. Damage may last for many years.

In the future there may be less harmful ways to exploit desert resources. One renewable resource that deserts have in abundance is solar power, because of the intense sunshine. At Luz in the Mojave Desert in California, solar panels spread across the landscape harness the sun's power. At present solar power is not economical because of the huge costs of setting up the solar panels.

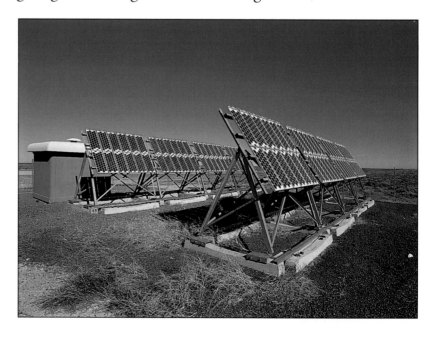

**Right** These solar panels provide electricity for telecommunications in the Australian Outback.

# 9. SPREADING DESERTS

**Left** Once a thriving oasis but now without a regular water supply, this abandoned city in northwest China is gradually being reclaimed by the desert.

At the margins of deserts, nature is delicately balanced; if the land is stripped of its vegetation it may not recover. Cutting down a tree is not just the loss of that tree but also the other plant life it supported by holding the soil together and providing shade. Without plant cover, water is less easily absorbed and runs off the land before it has a chance to soak in. There is nothing to stop the soil from being blown away and the land from turning into barren wasteland.

This process, called desertification, is occurring on the edge of some deserts. Wealthy countries can afford modern technology to find solutions, but in developing countries, where people live at subsistence levels and depend on the land, the effects of desertification can be disastrous.

**Below** Near the Namib Desert, the petrified remains of huge trees lie scattered around, a clue that the climate in this part of Africa must have once been much wetter.

In 1994 the United Nations Convention to Combat Desertification was signed, with the aim of protecting semiarid areas from desertification. The United Nations Environment Program claims that 900 million people worldwide and over 30 percent of the world's land area are affected by desertification. However, scientists argue about the extent of desertification, whether it is permanent, and why it is happening.

The world's climate naturally changes and can lead to the spread of deserts, but this happens slowly. Although there have been severe droughts since the 1970s, particularly in the Sahara and Sahel region, there is disagreement as to whether the climate changes are really long-term ones. Whether true or not, human activity is having greater and faster effects than natural changes.

## Natural changes

When the space shuttle *Columbia* took radar pictures of the Sahara, people were amazed by the photographs. Underlying the sand was a rocky landscape of hills and valleys cut by rivers at least 35 million years old. In the deserts of Arizona there is a petrified forest, fossils of giant prehistoric trees that grew 225 million years ago. It is probable that all the areas that are now desert were at one time well watered and covered by vegetation.

These changes are believed to be the result of climate changes caused by continental drift. The continents are very slowly but continually moving around the earth. Over periods of millions of years, the continents experience different climates. For instance, sandstones found in the Midlands in England are thought to be created from sand dunes that covered the area when it lay nearer the equator.

More recent climate changes have occurred because of the advance and retreat of polar ice; the periods when polar ice caps spread are known as ice ages. Over the last million years there have been ten major ice ages, making the world's climate alternately colder and warmer.

In the center of the Sahara, cave paintings made about eight thousand years ago have been discovered. These paintings show hunters with rhinoceroses, elephants, and antelopes; obviously at that time the area had wetter and cooler weather. The world's climate has been getting warmer since then, possibly resulting in the spread of some deserts, such as the Sahara. However, the warming of the earth has also brought a wetter climate to other parts of the world, so other deserts may be shrinking.

Farmers living in the semiarid regions around deserts in Africa depend on the little rain that falls every year to grow their crops. In recent years there have been long periods of drought in many of these regions. Crops have withered and died, leaving the people without food.

## Consequences of human activity

Global warming, the rise of the average temperature of the earth's atmosphere because of the vast quantities of fuel burned today, may be causing changes to deserts. Scientists cannot agree about the degree to which global warming is happening or the results it may bring. Many fear it is bringing changes in world climates and, in some places, encouraging the spread of deserts.

On the edge of deserts, the most immediate problems are the result of population growth and the way the land is farmed or otherwise used. Overgrazing is one major reason the land is becoming barren. There are many more people, and herds of cattle and goats are bigger than ever before. On large cattle ranches, there is insufficient rainwater or grass to sustain the animals, and goats are greedy eaters that demolish every bit of greenery in sight.

Although irrigation has greened some desert areas, it also has harmful effects. Without careful control and drainage, salinization can cause land to become barren, as a kind of salt desert. The growth in agriculture, especially where irrigated land is being used for cash crops, is pushing traditional herdsmen and poorer farmers onto

even less productive land. This puts further pressure on areas that can support only small numbers of people.

Semiarid areas are also being affected by the ever-increasing size of towns and cities and people's need for fuel. In those developing countries where people have to find firewood for cooking, trees and shrubs have been chopped down for hundreds of miles around towns, turning the surrounding land into desert.

## Controlling the spread

Sand dunes are slowly advancing to the edges of some deserts. To prevent sand from blowing onto farmland and villages, windbreaks are constructed of either artificial barriers or living plants. These windbreaks usually work only for the short term, because the wind gradually piles the sand up against the barrier and eventually covers it.

Planting shrubs and trees is the most common way of stabilizing soil and is a good long-term solution because when the soil is held in place by tree roots, other plants can take hold. In China, where the sands of the Gobi are being blown toward farmed and settled areas, straw mats have been placed on the dunes and small drought-resistant shrubs planted to hold the sand down. A long belt of trees, called the Great Green Wall, has also been planted; it not only acts as a windbreak but also provides a habitat that encourages other plants. Planting helps slow the spread of deserts as long as the young trees and shrubs are regularly watered, but it can be difficult and expensive to supply enough water in desert areas.

In semidesert areas, the numbers of grazing animals must be carefully controlled if the land is not to be reduced to a wasteland. For thousands of years, traditional methods, such as seasonal herding with small flocks, allowed land to recover.

Different cultivation methods can also help prevent land from turning into desert. Hillside terraces or low walls can stop what water there is from running off and causing soil erosion. They act like small dams by containing the water where it is needed. Planting crops in rows across slopes rather than down the hill also keeps water from running straight downhill. Research in the Sahara found that small piles of stones around plants help the soil to

Straw mats are used in China to hold shifting sand dunes in place. Small shrubs and grasses are planted between them, with the hope that they will take root permanently so that eventually there will be a thick cover of vegetation.

44

retain moisture. The development of more drought-resistant plants has also brought great benefits to desert regions.

Some of these solutions are simple and inexpensive and can be easily applied by local people themselves. This is particularly important in developing countries that do not have much money. There also have been many large-scale dam and irrigation projects to help people in semidesert areas, but to build them requires a great deal of money, which usually comes in the form of aid or loans from other countries.

Large projects may sometimes help, but often the people who are in greatest need lose out. For example, a project in Senegal to dam and irrigate the Senegal River valley has allowed more arid land to be farmed, but rich farmers have bought up the land to grow cash crops such as cotton and rice. Poorer farmers and traditional herdsmen cannot afford to buy the land and can no longer use pastures near the river where their animals once grazed in the dry season.

Experiences like these throughout the world have shown that it is often better to direct aid to local people, providing them with simple, cheap technology that they can apply and repair themselves. With careful management, desertification can be prevented in semiarid areas with their fragile environment. Applying farming and irrigation methods that desert dwellers already know and have used successfully may be one of the best solutions for the future.

In this Sahara oasis, low earth walls have been built around crops so water can be applied where it is most needed, without waste. This is a simple and inexpensive solution for farming in the desert.

# Glossary

**Amphibian**    A type of animal, such as a frog or a toad, that usually begins life in the water, breathing through gills, and later develops lungs and lives on land. Amphibians are cold-blooded creatures.

**Arid**    Dry.

**Aqueduct**    A large pipe used to bring water from a distant source.

**Aquifer**    An underground layer of rocks that contains water within the rocks' pores or joints.

**Barren**    Not producing vegetation.

**Bulbous**    Shaped like or having a bulb.

**Carnivores**    Meat-eating creatures.

**Cash crops**    Crops grown for sale rather than for local use.

**Contour plowing**    Plowing around a hill, not up and down, to prevent water runoff and erosion.

**Desertification**    The process by which desert is created, as a result of declining rainfall or misuse by people.

**Dormant**    Alive but not active or growing, as if asleep.

**Erode**    To wear away. Rocks and soil can be eroded by wind or water.

**Evaporation**    Water loss from soil and plants due to high temperatures.

**Exploit**    To make use of something in a productive and profitable way.

**Extinction**    The dying out of a species of plant, animal, or other living thing; the state of no longer existing.

**Fodder**    Coarse food, such as cornstalks and hay for cattle, sheep, and goats.

**Humid**    Moist or damp.

**Insulation**    Protection from heat or cold.

**Irrigation**    Watering the land artificially.

**Mammals**    Warm-blooded animals that feed their young on milk produced by the mother.

**Nocturnal**    Active at night.

**Nomads**    People who move from place to place, usually to find grazing for their animals.

**Overgraze**    To feed so many animals on grass that the land can no longer support them.

**Precipitation**    Rain, hail, and snow.

**Prey**    Animals that are captured and eaten by other animals.

**Reptiles**    Cold-blooded animals, such as lizards and snakes, that are covered with scales and usually lay eggs.

**Reservoir**    A place where water is collected and stored.

**Salinization**    the process of adding salt to the land, causing it to become so salty that plants can no longer grow.

**Sand dune**    A rounded hill or ridge of sand formed by the wind.

**Seasonal**    Something that happens only at certain times, or seasons, of the year.

**Staple food**    The main types of food eaten by humans.

**Strip mine**    A mine that is dug by removing large areas of the top surfaces of the land rather than digging underground tunnels to get at the minerals below the surface.

**Subsistence level**    A level of income that provides only the basic necessities of life, such as food, shelter, and water.

**Terraces**    Level areas cut into hillsides like steps to prevent water from flowing downhill.

**Tropical**    Characteristic of the Tropics (the area around the middle of the globe, between the Tropics of Cancer and Capricorn, on either side of the equator).

**Urine**    A liquid waste product that is discharged from an animal's body.

**Water table**    The level in the ground to which water drains.

**Weathering**    The action of wind, water, and extreme temperatures on the landscape.

# FURTHER READING

Bannan, Jan Gumprecht. *Sand Dunes.* Earth Watch. Minneapolis: Lerner Publications, 1989.

Bernard, Alan. *Kalahari Bushmen.* Threatened Cultures. New York: Thomson Learning, 1994.

Dixon, Dougal. *The Changing Earth.* Young Geographer. New York: Thomson Learning, 1993.

Fleisher, Paul. *Ecology A to Z.* New York: Dillon Press, 1994.

Flint, David. *The World's Weather.* Young Geographer. New York: Thomson Learning, 1993.

Lye, Keith. *Deserts.* Our World. New York: Silver Burdett, 1987.

McLeish, Ewan. *The Spread of Deserts.* Conserving Our World. Milwaukee: Raintree Steck-Vaughn, 1990.

MacQuity, Miranda.  *Desert.* Eyewitness Guides. New York: Alfred A. Knopf Books for Young Readers, 1994.

Mell, Jan. *Grand Canyon.* National Parks. New York: Crestwood House, 1988.

Sayre, April Pulley. *Desert.* Exploring Earth's Biomes. New York: Twenty-First Century Books, 1994.

Scoones, Simon. *The Sahara and its People.* People and Places. New York: Thomson Learning, 1993.

Twist, Clint. *Deserts.* Ecology Watch. New York: Dillon Press, 1991.

Watts, Barrie. *Twenty-Four Hours in a Desert.* Twenty-Four Hours. New York: Franklin Watts, 1991.

# FURTHER INFORMATION

For further information about animals and their habitats that are under threat, contact the following environmental organizations:

Center for Environmental Education, Center for Marine Conservation, 1725 De Sales Street NW, Suite 500, Washington, DC 20036

Friends of the Earth (U.S.A.), 218 D Street SE, Washington, DC 20003

Greenpeace U.S.A., 1436 U Street NW, Washington, DC 20009

World Wildlife Fund, 1250 24th Street NW, Washington DC 20037

These organizations all campaign to protect wildlife and habitats throughout the world.

**Picture acknowledgments**
Britstocke IFA/*Everts cover*, /F. Abraham 6; Mary Evans 35(lower); Eye Ubiquitous 18, 27(lower), /B. Adams 30, /H. Rogers 33(lower); Frank Lane Picture Agency /W. Wisniewski 4; NHPA /S. Dalton 21, /K. Switak 23(lower), /S. Krasemann 38(lower), /O. Rogge 40(lower); Still Pictures /C. Caldicott 9, /S. Fern 11(lower), /Denis-Huot 12, /M. Gunther 23(top), /Seitre 24(lower), /K. Raven 26, /M. Gilles 31, /W. Fautre 35(top), /M. Edwards 37(lower), 42, 43(lower), J. Roche 45; Tony Stone Worldwide /K. Stepnal 7, /G. Yeowell 11(top), /J. Cornish 13, /P. & K. Smith 15(lower), /P. Chesley 17, /G. Prentice 19(top), /J. Randklev 20(lower), /P. Chesley *title page*, & 19, /D. Hiser 32(lower), /P. Tweedie 37(top), /B. Edwards 38(top), 39, /J. Janqauax 43(top); J. Waterlow 8, 14, 16, 19(lower), 20(top), 24(top), 27(top), 29, 32(top), 33(top), 34, 36(top), 40(top), 42(both); Wayland Picture Library /G. Purcell 15(top), J. Waterlow 25, 28, *contents page*, & 32(top), 36(both), 44.
Maps and diagrams on pages 5, 7, 10, 12, 13, 17, 26, 29 by Peter Bull Design.

# Index

Numbers in **bold** refer to photographs